To
Kennedy Marie.

From
Grandma JoJo
First Easter
April 2012

Celebrate *the* Wonder *of* Little Girls

# Sugar & Spice
## AND EVERYTHING NICE

## CHRYS HOWARD

*Bestselling author of* HUGS FOR DAUGHTERS

# HOWARD BOOKS
### A DIVISION OF SIMON & SCHUSTER
New York   London   Toronto   Sydney

HOWARD
BOOKS

Published by Howard Books, a division of Simon & Schuster, Inc.
1230 Avenue of the Americas, New York, NY 10020
www.howardpublishing.com

Library of Congress Cataloging-in-Publication Data is available.

ISBN-13: 978-1-4165-7915-1
ISBN-10:     1-4165-7915-X

1  3  5  7  9  10  8  6  4  2

HOWARD and colophon are registered trademarks of Simon & Schuster, Inc.

Manufactured in China

For information regarding special discounts for bulk purchases, please contact:
Simon & Schuster Special Sales at 1-800-456-6798 or business@simonandschuster.com

Cover and interior design by Left Coast Design, Inc., Portland, OR 97229

*Time Out Ladies* by Dale Evans Rogers (Grand Rapids, MI: Fleming Revell,
a division of Baker Publishing Group, 1975). Used with permission.

Poem by Marcia Krugh Leaser. Used by Permission.

Scriptures quoted from *The Holy Bible, New Century Version*,
copyright © 1987, 1988, 1991 by Word Publishing, Dallas, Texas 75234. Used by permission.

To my sisters, Joneal and Jessi—

who shared the journey of girlhood with me

To my daughters, Korie and Ashley, and granddaughters,

Sadie, Macy, Ally, Aslyn, and Bella

who let me continue the journey

What are little boys made of?

What are little boys made of?

Frogs and snails

And puppy dog tails,

That's what little boys are made of.

What are little girls made of?

What are little girls made of?

Sugar and spice

And all things nice,

That's what little girls are made of.

ROBERT SOUTHEY

*English poet, 1774–1843*

# What are little girls made of?

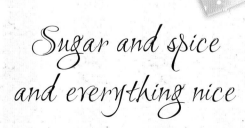

Sugar and spice
and everything nice

Sunshine and rainbows

and ribbons and hair bows

*Pink candy canes
and new Mary Janes*

God made the world with its towering trees,

Majestic mountains and restless seas.

Then paused and said, "It needs one more thing—

Someone to laugh and dance and sing,

To walk in the woods and gather flowers,

To commune with nature in quiet hours."

So God made little girls

With laughing eyes and bouncing curls,

With joyful hearts and infectious smiles,

Enchanting ways and feminine wiles.

And when He'd completed the task He'd begun,

He was pleased of the job He'd done.

For the world when seen though a little girl's eyes

Greatly resembles His own paradise.

ART KNIGHT

*Little girls are the nicest
things that can happen to people.
They are born with a little bit of
angel-shine about them, and though
it wears thin sometimes, there is always
enough left to lasso your heart—
even when they are sitting in the mud,
or crying temperamental tears,
or parading up the street
in Mother's best clothes.*

DALE EVANS ROGERS

# What are little girls made of?

Costumes and schemes
and magical dreams

I PRAISE YOU BECAUSE YOU MADE ME IN AN AMAZING AND WONDERFUL WAY. WHAT YOU HAVE DONE IS WONDERFUL. I KNOW THIS VERY WELL.

PSALM 139:14

Music and dance and taking a chance

A child to hold and cuddle,

'Tis a gift from God above.

And the world is so much brighter

When you have a child to love.

AUTHOR UNKNOWN

*God makes the world all over again*

*whenever a little child is born.*

JEAN PAUL RICHTER

# What are little girls made of?

Ponytails and hats and swinging a bat

Breezes and butterflies

*and raindrops from summer skies*

My feet were made to carry me

And how I love to run,

Past the garden and the gate,

Just soaking up the sun.

My hands were made to touch and feel,

Flowers, trees, and such.

I want to say, "Thank you, God,

For giving me so much."

CHRYS HOWARD

*Children have neither a past nor a future.*

*Thus they enjoy the present, which seldom happens to us.*

JEAN DE LA BRUYERE

What are little girls made of?

Giggles and grins and shopping with friends

*Sisters and treats*
*and matching bare feet*

He has put his angels in charge of you
to watch over you wherever you go.

PSALM 91:11

I'm not really sure

What I'll grow up to be.

But I know God has my plans–

He's holding them for me.

He's molding and He's shaping,

And I can't wait to see

The kind of person I'll become

And what God has planned for me.

Does He see me in a classroom

Teaching to the young?

Or maybe in a kitchen

Waiting supper to be done?

Does He see me at a hospital

Helping someone who needs care?

Or working in the beauty shop

Styling ladies' hair?

I guess I'll have to wait and see–

It's not as if I mind–

I'll gladly let God guide my steps

And follow close behind.

CHRYS HOWARD

*Keep your eyes on the stars and your feet on the ground.*

THEODORE ROOSEVELT

# What are little girls made of?

Tea parties and laces and baby-doll faces

High heels and hats

and fuzzy kitty cats

God gave me the greatest gift

in life He can bestow;

He granted me a child

and I was to help her grow.

I was to show her how to be happy

but not with what to play.

Teach her to express herself

but not of what to say.

I was to guide her each and every thought

yet: give her a will of her own.

Teaching to have great faith in God

she would reap what I had sown.

Yes, God gave me the greatest gift

and to Him I now must pray. . . .

"Please grant to me the strength I'll need

to watch her walk away."

MARCIA KRUGH LEASER

*A child is a beam of sunlight from the Infinite and Eternal,*

*with possibilities of virtue and vice—but as yet unstained.*

LYMAN ABBOTT

LET OUR DAUGHTERS BE
LIKE THE DECORATED
STONES IN THE TEMPLE.

PSALM 144:12

# What are little girls made of?

Hugs and kisses
and holiday wishes

*Laughter and love and blessings from above*

I have a friend in Jesus;

He's the best friend I know.

He walks and talks with me each day

And leads me as I go.

But sometimes I need to see

My Jesus with some skin.

It's then I know how blessed I am

That you became my friend.

CHRYS HOWARD

*Girls especially are fond of exchanging confidences with those whom they think they can trust; it is one of the most charming traits of a simple, earnest-hearted girlhood, and they are the happiest women who never lose it entirely.*

LUCY LARCOM

*A New England Girlhood*

THIS IS THE DAY THAT THE LORD HAS MADE.
LET US REJOICE AND BE GLAD TODAY!

PSALM 118:24

# What are little girls made of?

*Warm summer days and daddies who play*

Blankets and bears

*and sweet good-night prayers*

*That's what little girls are made of.*

Each second we live is a new and unique moment of the universe,

A moment that will never be again... and what do we teach our children?...

We should say to each of them: Do you know what you are?

You are a marvel. You are unique.

In all the years that have passed, there has never been another child like you.

Your legs, your arms, your clever fingers, the way you move.

You may become a Shakespeare, a Michelangelo, a Beethoven.

You have the capacity for anything. Yes, you are a marvel.

PABLO CASALS